A history
the 50th
holide

Gomerclarks
21/8/96

IMAGES OF

The Isle of Wight

IMAGES OF
The Isle of Wight

Donald A. Parr

The Breedon Books
Publishing Company
Derby

First published in Great Britain by
The Breedon Books Publishing Company Limited
Breedon House, 44 Friar Gate, Derby, DE1 1DA.
1996

ISBN 1 85983 044 7

Printed and bound by Butler & Tanner Ltd., Selwood Printing
Works, Caxton Road, Frome, Somerset.

Colour separations by Colour Services, Wigston, Leicester.

Jacket printed by Lawrence-Allen, Weston-Super-Mare, Avon.

Contents

Dedicated to
Melodina (Din-Din) Comendador
Spring 1996

Foreword

I FIRST met Don Parr some years ago when I was in a studio, surrounded by recording equipment, arranging music and editing some *Isle of Wight Legend* sound tapes with which he was particularly involved. He assured me that it was the first time he had watched a musician editing and was more than a little bewildered at the metres of waste sound tape surrounding my floor space. We became friends and have remained so ever since.

I was then and still am now incredulously impressed by Don's local historical knowledge combined with his ability to put it into print simply and readably so that it can be appreciated by young and old alike.

The Island, diverse in its history, is a place which infiltrates your very being, however long you have lived here. I am fortunate enough to have travelled and conducted in many of the world's exotic places and some, not quite so exotic, but every time, coming home is a pleasure because the soft green beauty found in Eire, the breathtaking Grand Canyon and Niagara in America and the mystery of Ayres Rock in Australia seem to be combined in miniature here on Wight.

No wonder our visitors return year after year. Most certainly *Images of the Isle of Wight* will enhance their enjoyment and add to their knowledge and I am proud to have been asked to write this short foreword

Peter T.G.White MA, AIGCM
Totland Bay, March 1996

Acknowledgements

The contents of this book cover a diverse area and include many hundreds of different people and subjects. It would have been a much more difficult task but for the generosity, patience and assistance of a great many people, not least the publishers. Therefore, may I thank the following: Ralph Abbott; Valerie Attrill of Cowes; Gwen Best of Niton; Marian and Brian Blake, landlords of Raffles Tavern, Bembridge; Paul Cooper of Freshwater; Cowes Amateur Operatic & Dramatic Society; Cowes Salvation Army; Bert Draper of Newport; Mrs J.Fripp of Cowes; Godshill County Primary School; 'Chick' Hickling of Cowes; Dr Insole of Sandown; J.Lavers of Apse Heath; Audrey Moore of Shanklin; Olive Newington of Niton; Miss M.Nicholson of Chale Green; Bill Patten of Whitwell; Phoebe Riddings of Yarmouth; 'EG' Rapkins of Yaverland; St Boniface County Primary School; P.South of Cowes; Vera Taylor of Cowes; Brian Thatcher of Shanklin; Anne Toms, director of the Quay Arts Centre Gallery; Newport, Ventnor Cricket Club; Westland Aerospace, East Cowes; West Wight Football Club, Freshwater; David White, photographer of Cowes; the family of the late Jim Whittington of Wroxall; Wroxall County Primary School.

My thanks also to my friends Simon Dabell, director of Blackgang Chine Theme Park, Blackgang; Tony Polino of Roma Taxis of Newport; Wayne Pritchett, harbour master, Newport; Bill Shepard of Newport; and Peter T.G.White for the foreword and his general assistance.

Introduction

PLACES mean something to us. Just what they do mean is dependent on the experiences we have. It was Karl Marx who wrote to Friedrich Engels in July 1874 stating, 'The Island is a little paradise,' although Charles I was purported to have said, "And I gave up paradise for this Island."!

Whether our jobs necessitate us travelling or whether we simply use our annual holidays to enjoy a new location, either at home or abroad, the fact remains that places really do mean something to us. We may be a member of that vast army who return to the same area time after time, or one of those who are quite content to remain at home. The positive or negative thoughts we have are resultant entirely on the pleasant, or even in some instances, unpleasant observations we make whilst we are there.

It is unusual to hear negative comments about the Isle of Wight from visitors or even residents. Karl Marx was obviously very happy when he made that remark to Engels, but the unfortunate Charles, imprisoned at Carisbrooke Castle, would have associated the Island with the ever-looming inevitable. Who can blame the poor man for not being enamoured? Quotes, then, from two famous people, one positive and one negative, just two sides of an oft-tossed coin.

Many well-known artistes from the world of radio, television, dance, acting, music and comedy have made their homes on the island, together with some who are not so welcome but are sent here as a penury measure to our three prisons. Most of the more notable criminals spend a while either at Parkhurst or Albany jails.

Through the years many noted figures in English history have been frequent visitors to the Isle of Wight, quite a number with a literary bent such as Charles Dickens, Algernon Swinburn, John Keats, Lord George Byron, and William Wordsworth to name but a few. Author J.B.Priestley decided to make the Island his home and having rented Billingham Manor at Chillerton for a while, purchased Brook Hill House at Brook and lived there for the rest of his life. Poet Laureate, Alfred Lord Tennyson, also became domicile here, having purchased Farringford House in Freshwater.

Tennyson became a good friend of Queen Victoria and Albert, Prince Consort, both of whom lived for most of the year at Osborne House, East Cowes, a house designed by Albert in Palladian style and resembling an Italian villa. The Royal couple were disenchanted with the hustle and bustle of London and Brighton and wanted to be near the sea and the yachting scene. Prince Albert died in 1861 and the Queen died at Osborne 40 years later, in 1901.

In 1878, when taking a walk along the cliff above Sandown Bay, a very young Winston Churchill saw the Naval training ship HMS *Eurydice* sink at Dunnose Point with the loss of many lives. Throughout his long and eventful career he often recalled the incident and told how the memory of it left an indelible mark.

The waters surrounding the Isle of Wight, the English Channel at the south and the Solent at the north, have always been treacherous and at times extremely rough – a nightmare for mariners and ships navigators, be they in charge of small pleasure craft or large commercial liners or tankers. But for the vigilance of the Trinity House personnel who maintain the two lighthouses at St Catherine's and the Needles, pilot boats and the HM Coastguard service, many more ships would be lost on the rocks. Praise must also be given now and throughout the ages to the gallant men of the Royal National Lifeboat Institution and The Inshore Rescue Service, who put to sea in all weathers, risking their own lives, to go to the aid of those in distress. Neither must we forget the newer addition of the equally courageous Air Sea Helicopter Rescue Service.

During World War Two, the Island played a large role in the invasion by Britain of occupied Europe. Not only was it a dormitory island and training area, but also the setting for PLUTO or Pipe Line Under the Ocean. This was the brainchild of the late Lord Louis Mountbatten, later to become Governor of the Island. The idea for PLUTO, one of the most successful of the war, was that when the planned British invasion took place, a steel and rubber pipe was placed along the sea bed from Shanklin Chine to France and used to pump the much needed petroleum spirit not only just to the beachheads, but as the advance gathered momentum, so PLUTO went with them. With the cessation of hostilities, PLUTO was rewound on to drums and salvaged with very little loss.

Leaving the coast and travelling inland we see many fine manor houses, most of which are still open to the public but some alas, are no more, having been subjected to crumbling and erosion over the years or even demolition. One such grand edifice dating back to the 12th century was situated at Knighton and was the home of Sir Hugh de Merville, one of the four knights who assassinated Sir Thomas à Beckett at Canterbury Cathedral in 1170. The house was later to become the property of Sir Ralph de Gorge and became known as Knighton Gorges. From then it continued as a gentleman's residence and after additions was classed as one of the finest Elizabethan manor houses in the land. The last owner in the early 1800s was Capt Bissett, well known for his involvement in a well-publicised court case when he eloped with the wife of Sir Richard Woresley from Appuldurcombe. Although Worseley won his case, he was awarded one shilling (5p) damages. Just prior to his death in 1821, Capt Bissett had the house demolished to stop it falling into the hands of his daughter who had married against his wishes.

Another manor of consequence in the centre of the Island is Arreton Manor. There has been a manor house on this site since the time of King Alfred, who mentioned it in his will. The present building dates from 1595 and is now open to the public and a place well worth visiting.

In this book I have tried to show life on the Island from the late 1800s until the modern day. From the snows of 1881 to the floods of the 1960s. From the early steam buses to the modern double-decker diesel monsters which roam our towns and countryside today.

The charm of the Island landscape lies in its variety and the astonishing range of its contrasting scenery, from the rugged coastline of the southern shores to the long series of landslips near Blackgang Chine brought about by rain water seeping through the upper layers of soft clays and sand and causing them to slide over the heavy gault clay appropriately called 'Blue Slipper'. This disturbance of earth encourages the growth of plantains, food for the Island's rare butterfly, the Granville Fritillary. The appearance of the Island has been shaped over the centuries by man clearing the downs to graze his sheep, coppicing the woodlands for fencing material and quarrying the stone to build his houses. This Island, famous for its downland walks, its copses full of wild daffodils, primroses and bluebells spreading scented carpets beneath oak trees, is a joy for all who come to share its beauty.

Donald A. Parr.
Totland Bay, Isle of Wight
March 1996

Places

St Boniface Down, Ventnor in 1930 showing Southern Vectis Coaches.

St James Square, Newport, in 1966.

Calbourne Pump in 1904 situated at the junction of Lynch Lane and School Lane.

Another view of Calbourne Pump taken in 1927.

Church Road, Shanklin, taken from a glass plate negative by J.Dore. The following four photographs are by the same photographer and are all dated 1869.

Another photograph of Shanklin, this time Sampson's stationery shop.

A lobster fisherman's cottage at Ventnor.

A gentleman's residence on Shanklin Undercliff.

A fisherman's family at Luccombe.

St James Square, Newport, at the turn of the century, showing the weekly cattle market.

Another view of the market in St James Square, showing the drinking fountain.

Pier approach at Ryde in the 1920s. Note the variety of vehicles in the picture.

The Guildhall, Newport, prior to 1870. The present clock tower was added later.

An early picture of Way Ridett auction rooms in Newport.

Early woodcut print of St Thomas Square and Church, Newport.

Newport Old Quay between the swing
bridge and Coppins Bridge in 1905.

Simeon Monument pictured in 1905, situated at the junction of Castle Road and Carisbrooke Road. The house behind the monument was known as 'Little Gatcombe'.

Carisbrooke High Street in 1899.

The Priory and Church, Carisbrooke, in 1893.

This monument near Blackgang is known locally as 'The Alexandrian Pillar' (or 'Hoy's Monument'). It was erected by businessman Michael Hoy to commemorate the visit to Britain in 1814 of Tsar Alexander I of Russia. Subsequently, W.H.Dawes, who resented such respect to the Tsar, placed a plaque on the north face of the pillar's base in memory of British troops who fell in the Crimean War.

Niton High Street in 1930. Baverstock's, the local grocer, draper and milliner, was the main source for shopping until the early 1970s. It is now owned by the Norris family.

An aerial view of the River Medina and East Cowes, showing the ferry terminal and British Hovercraft factory (now Westland Aerospace). The large Union Flag was painted on the main hanger door in 1976 to celebrate the Queen's forthcoming Silver Jubilee.

Trinity Road in Ventnor 1924. Viewing the scene, it is as if time had stood still.

In the 1940s this cottage in Godshill was owned by Mrs Vapini and was known as 'The Show Cottage'. Included among the many visitors were Queen Mary and Princess Beatrice. Glass tubes were suspended from the ceiling into which visitors would be asked to deposit sixpence. The cottage dates back to the 1500s.

This rare picture of the main road from Shanklin to Godshill was taken in 1897.

The imposing Hazlewood residence in Ashey Road, Ryde, was destroyed by a direct hit in an air raid during World War Two. Prior to that it had been a private house and latterly, Ryde Youth Hostel.

Bonchurch Pond, Bonchurch, Ventnor, in 1902. This rare photograph was taken from a glass plate by Island photographer J.Dore.

Ventnor Esplanade taken in 1890.

Another view of Ventnor in 1911, showing Belgrove Road.

Ventnor Chest Hospital, now demolished and the site used as the home of Ventnor Botanical Gardens.

The Undercliff Hotel at Niton, destroyed by enemy action during World War Two.

This cottage in Newchurch was known as 'Canteen Cottage' due to it being used in 1800 by German troops stationed in the village during the Napoleonic threat.

Newchurch village in 1875.

The Tea Rooms at Brook. An interesting feature of this small West Wight hamlet is that the Post Office comes to Brook and uses a caravan as an office for the day.

The Carnegie Free Library in Sandown.

East Cowes Town Hall, at one time the centre of municipal administration for East Cowes. With the merging of East and West Cowes in 1895 it became redundant. It was then used as a theatre for many years and is now a community centre.

The Shell House in Cambridge Road, East Cowes was presented by Queen Victoria as a wedding present to William Attrill. This act of generosity by the Queen was in gratitude for him teaching the Prince of Wales (Edward VII) some manners. As a youngster the Prince kicked over a tray containing William's periwinkles which he was selling. In return William blacked his eye.

Newport High Street just after World War Two, showing the Ist Newport Old Guard Scout Band.

Cowes High Street showing the war memorial prior to its removal to the grounds of Northwood House. This memorial sustained heavy damage during World War Two but was carefully restored.

Cowes High Street during the early part of the century.

The Mill House, Yarmouth, showing the breakwater which halted the flow of water into the one time safe anchorage of Draft Haven.

St Helen's Tide Mill closed in 1931 and fell into disrepair. It was further damaged by an incendiary bomb during the last war. The mill was subsequently demolished and a private dwelling now stands on the site.

The open air swimming pool Newport which was situated in Seaclose Recreation Ground. The pool opened in 1936 and was to remain the only swimming pool in the area until its recent closure.

Sherratt's electrical store, situated at the top of Newport High Street, was destroyed by fire on 22 May 1962.

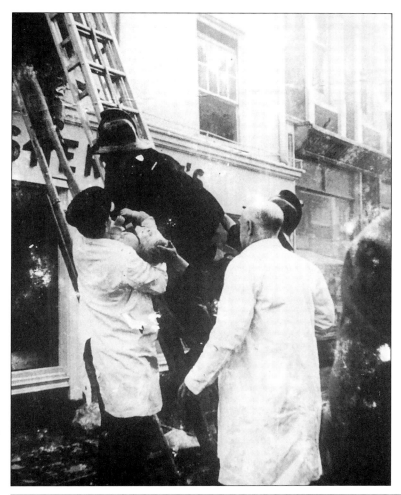

During the blaze at Sherratt's, fireman Alf Phillips rescued a small child, while ambulance driver Charlie Harvey waited for the infant who was unharmed.

The Grantham Hotel, Cowes, overlooking the Solent.

Cowes High Street in 1911.

The main road at Godshill in 1913.

Wheeler's Bay, near Blackgang, at the turn of the century when it was well known for its fishing industry. Pictured are the fishermens' huts and the net drying poles of the mackerel fishermen.

Cowes Green, showing the Flora statue next to the bandstand.

The River Yar at Alverstone. Between the two world wars it was popular with those who enjoyed a little rowing or canoeing on a quiet Sunday afternoon.

No one accuses Island authorities of lacking compassion.

The Wheeler family in 1900 enjoying a summer on the beach and repairing their nets and tackle in readiness for the coming season.

An early picture of the Wheeler family taken in 1879 in Wheeler's Bay, named after them because they had been fishing there for hundreds of years. Although quite a respected family, this shows the spartan conditions under which they lived.

The Folly Inn at Whippingham started life in 1752 as a beached barque used for serving refreshments for those travelling up-river to Newport Quay. Until the early 1880s, part of the keel was in the main bar but its whereabouts is now unknown. The name 'Folly' is presumed to be derived from the name of the original barque *Les Follies*.

The Crab Inn at Shanklin in 1906. The man in the doorway is the grandson of the landlord at the time and the girl is the barmaid.

Newport High Street in the 1930s.

Ventnor High Street, believed to be in 1891.

Newport Harbour in 1890 prior to the erection of buildings. On the extreme right of the photograph is the newly-built fencing of Fairlee Cemetery.

Shalfleet Village in the 1890s.

The Royal Pier Hotel prior to its demolition. The photograph is taken from seaward and shows the Esplanade Fountain and formal gardens.

The Falcon Hotel, Swanmore Road, Ryde, in 1880. The Falcon is still a popular hotel today.

Whitwell High Street in the early 1920s.

The Painter's Arms public house in Cowes.

Fountain Pier, Cowes, in the late 1970s. At one time it was the main port of entry for Red Funnel Steamers from Southampton, but with the enlargement of the facilities at East Cowes for roll on/roll off vessels, this pier is now used for the hydrofoil service.

St Mary's Mission Hall situated in St Andrew's Street in the 1950s. St Mary's Mission was built and opened in 1886 and still is used today as a community centre.

High Street, Cowes, in the mid-1980s, at the junction with Market Hill.

York Street, Cowes. A typical example of three storey Victorian style houses.

These two photographs of Shooter's Hill, Cowes, were taken on a Sunday morning in the winter of 1985.

Birmingham House, Cowes, was built in 1752 by William Arnold, collector of customs at East Cowes. The plaque on the wall denotes the fact that his son, Thomas was born there in 1795. Thomas Arnold, author of *Tom Brown's Schooldays*, became headmaster of Rugby School in 1828 and developed it into one of Britain's greatest public schools.

Cowes High Street at the turn of the century.

The Royal Yacht Squadron at Cowes in 1892.

This photograph, originally taken from a glass plate, is of Cowes Green and thought to date from the 1870s. Cowes Green was donated to the town by George Robert Stephenson, nephew of George Stephenson, inventor of *The Rocket* and pioneer of the railway system.

Pinings Corner in Yarmouth High Street, now the home of Phoebe Raddings, was in need of a 'face lift'. When the exterior coating of plaster was removed in May 1995 it revealed the name of one of the original occupiers of the premises.

Godshill School in 1924.

G.M.Taylor, bakers and confectioners, with their delicacies at the Shanklin Show.

The Pond at Bonchurch in 1913.

The Royal Hotel first opened its doors in 1832. As most of the customers arrived by boat, the hotel would send down horses for the guests and the boat men would carry their baggage up to the hotel. Queen Victoria was a frequent visitor to the Hotel.

This early photograph shows a farmer carting hay from his farm near Shorwell to Newport cattle market.

An early photograph of St Boniface School, Ventnor, taken before the hills in the background were planted with trees.

An aerial photograph of the mouth of the River Medina at Cowes.

The Hare and Hounds public house at Gallows Chute, Newport. Inside are displayed the gruesome remains of Michael Morey who murdered his grandson.

East Cowes Esplanade. It was opened in 1924 by Mr George Sheddon who donated the land to build the esplanade to relieve unemployment in East Cowes.

The memorial to ten-year-old John Valentine Grey, murdered by his employer, Benjamin Davies, the town sweep, in 1822.

During the 1980s and 1990s, Cowes underwent many changes and many of the older buildings such as schools and the railway station, were demolished. This is quite a modern photograph of the excavation for the building of the new Co-op Supermarket.

The old West Cowes Town Hall at the junction of Market Hill, demolished in the late 1940s. The site was for many years a car park until being used for housing in the 1980s.

The Priory at Nettlestone, now a fashionable hotel, dates back to the 16th century. In 1927 it was purchased by an American lady who was so enchanted with everything English that she changed her name to 'St George'. This famous porch dating from the 14th century she had imported from France and rebuilt, brick by brick, adding the sculpture of St George on his horse.

People

Cowes Salvation Army Band in 1907. Featured from left to right, commencing in the rear row, are C.Slade, W.Martin, 'Dad' Blake, W.Carpenter, H.Carpenter, W.Carter, W.Souter, H.Russell, F.Martin, S.Burton, B.Payne, A.Adams, A.Davis, B.Powell, F.Wootton, H.Dunford, C.Burton, W.Chiverton, A.Davis (bandmaster), Mrs Hill, 'Ensign' Hill, W.Duffett, J.Carter and S.Dunford.

The Island MP in 1905, J.Seely, later to become the first Lord Mottistone, arriving in St James Square, Newport, to open the new drinking fountain.

During World War Two the Southern Vectis Bus Company formed their own Home Guard unit. Those included here are Reg Hayles, Waven Whale, Jack Beasley, R.Blee, S.Bartlett, Sid Tosdevin, W.Blee and Bert Reynolds.

The Newport Home Guard MT Platoon in 1944.

At the turn of the century, the Revd J.M.Banford of Newchurch introduced an annual pageant of Queen and Beauty in the village. The photograph shows the 1908 pageant in full swing.

The Island MP Douglas Hall visits the Newchurch pageant. He is pictured here with 'Skipper' Clark, headmaster of the village school, in 1912.

St James Square, Newport, in 1890. Leaning against the lamp-post was a much-loved figure. Because of his disability – he was a deaf mute – he was known as 'Dummy', an acceptable nickname at that time.

Cowes Town Band in 1931, pictured in the grounds of Northwood House, Cowes. Included are Bill Fripp, Art Dyer, Jim Jones, Reg Crouch and bandmaster Freddy Smart.

Sue Ryder OBE on a visit to the Island to raise funds for the Cheshire Homes.

Sommerton, near Cowes, had its own airfield until the 1950s. Pictured here in 1950 are Jimmy Raddings, his wife, Phoebe and dog Liebling with their Auster aircraft.

Remembrance Day Parade, School Green Road, Freshwater, in 1950. Phoebe Raddings proudly carries the standard for the British Red Cross.

The West Wight British Red Cross preparing their float for the Newport Carnival in 1958.

The Crab Inn, Shanklin, in 1959 showing Maureen James, Gladys Bunn, George Bunn and Patrick Jefferies.

Not all our Island visitors are welcome as this photograph shows. Peter Sutcliffe 'The Yorkshire Ripper', arrives at Newport Court to give evidence after being attacked whilst serving part of his life sentence at Parkhurst Prison.

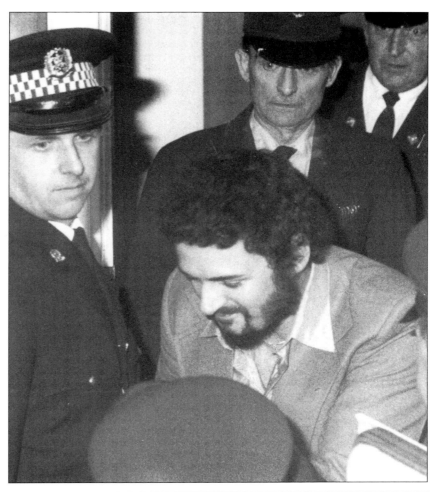

Inmates of Albany Prison protesting and airing their grievances by climbing on to the roof in 1983.

Far left: This picture, taken in the 1920s, shows the speed king Kay Don on his powerboat in Cowes Harbour.

Left: Sir Max Aitken on board his cruiser *Blue Max* with his wife in 1976.

Jeremy Thorpe MP visiting the Island on an election campaign.

The 1st Sandown Isle of Wight Sea Scouts was to form the Cliff Rescue Service which for many years, including throughout World War Two, served as an emergency rescue service. Pictured here with their Ford motor car in 1951, the year they won the Scouts' Silver Medal for Gallantry, are (left to right) D.Pain, C.W.Dibbens, K.V.Brett and K.I.Hooper.

Another picture of the Cliff Rescue Service, showing a close-up of the standard equipment they carried, including the large rope ladder, stretcher, lifebelts and lamps. This time again pictured with the faithful Ford car are (left to right) W.J.Robinson, A.E.Booth and W.G.Travers.

1st East Cowes Girls Life Brigade in 1928. Elsie James was president of the unit, a position she held until her death aged 101. Pictured here are L.Baird, L.Haliday, Mrs Waite, W.Barnes, M.Slade, W.Barton, M.Love, L.Smith, K.Lawrence, E.Howes, D.Moore, E.Lawrence, O.Lowen, I.Ackland, C.Edwards, H.Adams, M.Adams, A.Crozier, J.Knight, Mrs A.Fryer, M.Flemming, G.Bell, M.Bettridge, O.Merrifield, L.Gutteridge, E.Gnazell, B.Dove, B.Lawrence, M.Trevis, E.Barton, D.Attwater and M.Saunders.

Capt Adams-Connor, lord lieutenant of the Isle of Wight, county president of the Royal British Legion and Isle of Wight chief constable with British Legion poppy sellers at Cowes War Memorial in 1932.

Shanklin firemen with their newly-acquired steam engine in 1907.

Unfortunately, we are unable to ascertain the name of the coach driver who, it seems, has been invited to join the gnomes of Blackgang Chine for a game of cards in 1950.

Newchurch Village children in 1914 taking part in the ancient custom of shroving.

The Newport annual Wool Fair was held at The Rink, situated off Lugley Street, where fleeces would be auctioned. The picture dates from 1910.

In common with most towns during World War Two, East Cowes had its own Civil Defence first-aid party. Included here are Messrs Steed, Tiltman, Maegek, Chambers, South, Watts, Washbrook, Simpson, Raper, Walkinshaw, Old and Small.

Arthur William (Bob) Timms, outside his wet fish shop in Ryde 1962.

A group at Cowes railway station in 1948. They are believed to be the host families of Czechoslovakian children who had been staying in Cowes after the war. Included are Mrs J.Fripp, Mr W.Fripp, Miss Margaret Fripp and Florrie Rudkins.

J.Milne, well known early Island photographer and seismologist, pictured at Niton Undercliff from a glass plate negative taken in 1902.

Fishermen landing their catch on Shanklin beach in 1901.

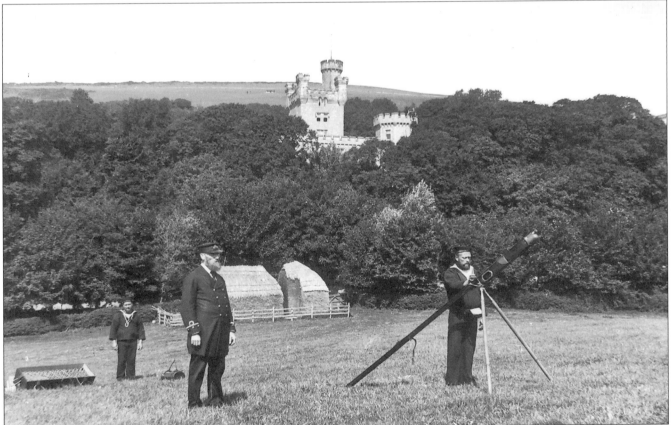

In the early days of the coastguard, rocket drill included the setting up of sheer legs and rope ways. These were used to practise the movement of men and equipment over long distances on cliff tops and rugged terrain. These four photographs *(also overleaf)*, taken by Mr J. Dore in 1900 and using the old glass plate camera, give us a good insight into the vigorous training which these men undertook at Steephill.

As detailed on the previous page, training at Steephill.

As part of their therapy, patients at the Royal National Chest Hospital at Ventnor were encouraged to work in the open air. Here are a group of chaps working in the grounds. Patients with chest complaints would often have to spend a year in hospital and with some, this soon became a way of life.

The Flora Statue now standing in the grounds of Northwood House, Cowes, was unveiled in 1980 by Mr and Mrs Ward, whose family presented it to the Council in 1926. Pictured with this statue they so lovingly restored are pupils of Love Lane School including Margaret Lennox, Sharee Hughes, Tony Gildant, Naomi Ashley, Kirsty Harower, Katherine Wellstead and, with her hand resting on the arm of the statue, Joanne Higginson.

In 1981 many small containers and large drums of corrosive and dangerous chemicals were washed up along Island beaches.

So hazardous were these chemicals that a special squad was brought in to deal with the situation.

When the clean up was completed the beaches were toured to ensure all was safe for the holiday season.

East Cowes Infants School, 1920. Among the pupils are Betty Church, Alan Dexter, Roy Street, Bill March, Bill Davies, Robert Stevens, Dorothy Parsons, Dorothy Arnold, Gilbert James, Margaret Herbert, Alan Ford, James Orchard, Bill South, Phyliss Sinnicks, Bill Moth, Olive Blake, Jack Corny, Jocelyn Hendy, Betty Ford, Norah Nicholson, Peggy Snudden, Sylvia Barton, Ted Reed, Marjorie Lawrence and Eric Tiltman. The teacher is Mrs Ford.

Wroxall Sunday School children pictured in their Sunday best in 1910. The teacher (back left) is Mr Newnham.

Wroxall School orchestra in 1905 with teacher Mr Francis. Two identified young violinists are Annie Morris and Lillian Whittington.

A portrait of George 'Jolly' Saunders taken in a Newport studio in 1918. George, a much loved Niton personality, died in 1938 at the age of 82.

Entertainment

In 1957 a group of ballet students visited the Isle of Wight to demonstrate various aspects of dance to schoolchildren. Hilary White shows the balance and co-ordination of a professional.

Rick Wakeman, international musician and TV star, pictured in 1993 after a performance of *The Gospels* at Cowes. Rick is shown here meeting Cowes singing student, 14-year-old Emily Renshaw.

Also working as narrator of *The Gospels* on that occasion was Ian Lavender, better known to millions as Private Pike in BBC television's *Dad's Army*.

At the end of their term of apprenticeship at Saunders Roe it was the custom for the youngsters to stage a play. Here in 1956 some of them are seen in a production of the farce *Seagulls Over Sorento*.

The Cowes Amateur Operatic and Dramatic Society, known locally as CAODS, in their production of *The Rebel Maid* in April 1931.

CAODS again, this time six years later during a performance of the Gilbert and Sullivan operetta *HMS Pinafore*. Among the cast are Sidney Rayner, Harry Wellspring, Edgar Manning, Phil Jones, Sydney Sheath, Adrian Scadding, George Waring Jnr, Norah Marshall, Peggy Scadding and Doris Payton.

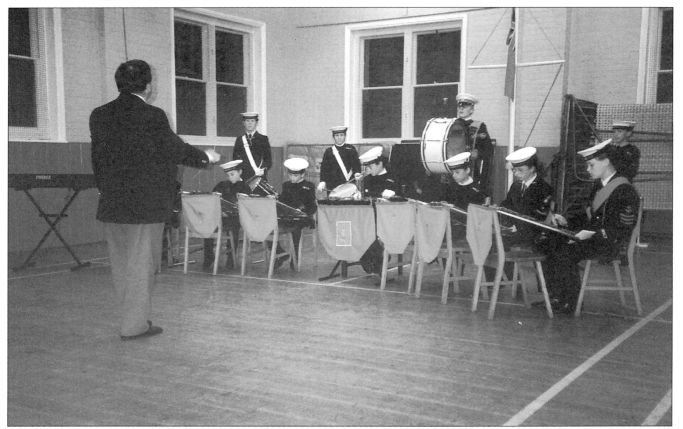

Part of the band of the Isle of Wight Nautical Cadet Force in 1992 being put through their paces by conductor and musical director, Peter White. Included are Sarah and Melissa Gardner, Vicky Jones, Clare Vivash, Richard Gardner and Richard Evans (bass drum).

The Alexander Hall was situated in Birmingham Road, Cowes and was the home of CAODS from 1911 to 1939. One of the last performances there was *The Gondoliers* by Gilbert and Sullivan.

The cast of CAODS production of *Les Cloches de Cornville* staged in 1922. Here they are pictured enjoying a well-earned outing.

Royalty

Osborne House showing the Palladian style of the building, somewhat resembling an Italian villa. The Royal couple would be in residence during July and August and December to February. It was originally the property of Lady Isabella Blanchford. In 1845 Queen Victoria, who wanted a home away from the bustle of Brighton and the noise of London, bought this 1,000 acres of land and Albert, Prince Consort, completely redesigned the existing building and extended it. One year later the Royal couple were able to move in to one of the wings.

King Alphonse of Spain, pictured here in Newport after winning a shooting contest in 1912. He married Princess Ena, daughter of Princess Beatrice and granddaughter of Queen Victoria.

During her long reign a landing stage was constructed for Queen Victoria at the Trinity House HQ in East Cowes. In 1922 it was moved to Newport and converted into a bungalow.

The Duke of Edinburgh demonstrating his skills to Prince Charles and Uffa Fox in the Solent in 1962.

Her Majesty, Queen
Elizabeth, the Queen
Mother talking to Mary
Saunders, Mayor of
Ventnor, at the opening of
the Botanical Gardens.

The late Lord Louis Mountbatten,
Governor of the Isle of Wight, pictured
on one of his visits to the Botanical
Gardens at Ventnor.

Many Newport residents turned out in St James Square in 1902 to witness the laying of the foundation stone of the memorial to Queen Victoria. As a mark of respect the square was lined with fir trees tied to the surrounding railings.

King George V pictured at Atherfield.

Prince Edward takes to the water at Cowes on his first sailing lesson.

Queen Victoria sitting in the stern of her Royal Yacht at Trinity landing stage Cowes before returning to the mainland.

The Royal Yacht prepares to weigh anchor and the royal salute is sounded.

Britannia proceeding through Cowes harbour to the open sea.

Cowes High Street was bedecked with flags to welcome Queen Victoria as she paraded through the streets in a open carriage on the occasion of her Diamond Jubilee in 1897.

After the Diamond Jubilee procession had passed along Cowes High Street, the crowd still followed their beloved Queen.

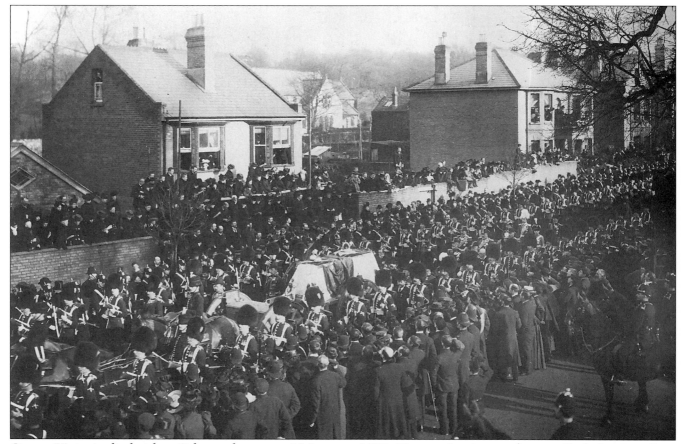

Queen Victoria died at her Osborne home on 22 January 1901. Her cortège is seen here at York Avenue, East Cowes, at the start of its journey to Westminster Abbey and the Lying-in-State.

Churches

St Boniface Church, Bonchurch, in 1900.

The Old Church, St Boniface at Bonchurch *c.*1922. Tradition states that the monks of Lyre first landed at Monks Bay in the eighth century and founded the first Church of St Boniface at Bonchurch, or as it was then known, Bonecerce. A coin of Aethelwulf, father of Alfred the Great, was found there.

Roud Baptist Church in 1921. First opened in 1859 it was closed during World War One but later reopened. It finally closed in 1971.

The Parish Church of All Saints', Godshill, as it looked in 1930.

Lightning struck Godshill Church on 14 January 1904, damaging the tower. The interior of the church also suffered severe damage as this picture shows.

Interior of St Luke's Chapel at the Royal National Hospital, Ventnor. Some of the stained-glass windows were removed before demolition in the 1960s. These were resited in St Lawrence Old Church and re-dedicated in the presence of Queen Elizabeth, the Queen Mother.

St Thomas Church, Newport, in 1993 undergoing repairs to the tower.

St James Church, Ryde, erected in 1827, has been described by an eminent architectural historian as 'a priceless period piece of early 19th-century Anglican Church arrangement and furnishings'. Very few specimens of this type of church have survived.

St Blazius Church, Shanklin, pictured in the snow on 30 December 1908.

Methodist Church and school, Birmingham Road, Cowes. Opened on 6 June 1901, it combined with Mill Hill Methodist Church in the 1960s.

St Mildred's Church, Whippingham, known as Queen Victoria's Church, was designed by Albert, Prince Consort, and is the resting place of Princess Beatrice and Prince Henry of Battenberg.

The parish church of All Saints' Freshwater in 1904.

Built in 1614, this church, dedicated to St James can be seen in The Square at Yarmouth. It replaced the church which was situated at the far end of the town and destroyed by the French.

St Andrew's Church, Norton. At one time it was the garrison church serving Fort Victoria and Golden Hill Fort but with the closure of the military establishments and falling congregations, the church amalgamated with others and the building was sold. It is now a private dwelling.

The thatched church of St Agnes at Freshwater Bay, one of the few thatched churches in the south.

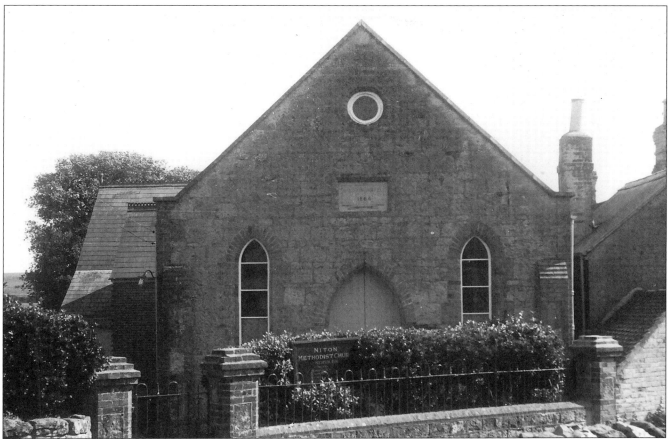

Niton Methodist Church was built in 1863. Local builders were invited to tender to undertake the work and the winning tender was that of Messrs Moses & Walden of Ventnor. For building a church with a seating capacity for 100 their cost was £181 10s 0d. This was accepted on 26 October 1863.

All Saints, Newchurch, with its wooden tower. It is one of the oldest churches on the Island.

The Easter Monday outing from Roud Chapel in 1921. Included in the picture are Harry Brennon, Mrs Plumbley, Mrs Butcher, Mrs Lacy, Mr and Mrs Tutton, Miss Gird, Arthur Attril, Mrs McCumley from Wroxall and Olive Saunders. The chapel was opened in 1859.

Roud Baptist Chapel decorated for Harvest Festival in 1956. Unfortunately, in common with many country places of worship, it was forced to close in 1971 after giving 112 years' service to the Baptist Church and the local community.

Weather

An exceptionally high tide at East Cowes on 27 November 1924 caused severe flooding.

Water rose by three or four feet, causing extensive damage to shops in the vicinity.

Flooding at Medina Road, West Cowes, on 11 December 1910.

Some good samaritans helping their neighbours.

The severe snow storms of 1881 were the worst in the Island's recorded history. This photograph shows the snow at Daish's Corner, Shanklin.

The snow of 1881 also caused great havoc in Newport High Street.

Snow often visits the Island but normally only in small amounts as these pictures of Shanklin in the 1980s show. Thoroughfares, such as Victoria Avenue in the first picture, were soon gritted and cleared.

The floods in 1960 were the worst on record. The River Medina burst its banks in many places. Here is Shide Path at the height of the flooding.

Jimmy Raddings, of Braxton Lodge, Yarmouth, had difficulty in digging his way out to Hallet Chute.

Not everyone escapes the occasional snow as this Southern Vectis bus shows when it was stranded in 1952. Left to right are Messrs Watkins, Cheverton, Daish, Nelson, Hayles and Chatfield.

This unusual photograph of our 'Sunshine Isle' shows a pattern of icicles at the window of Braxton Lodge, Yarmouth, in 1954.

On The Land

A threshing gang at Newchurch in 1900 with Alfred and Nathan Smith.

A threshing gang pictured at Winford in 1930. They would move from farm to farm.

Vic Hiscock, the village thatcher, at Newchurch in 1950.

The Isle of Wight hunt at Newchurch in 1906. In those days, whenever possible any hunt meet would be followed by the ladies in their carriages.

Mr Mackett making ladders at Newchurch in the early 1900s.

Milkmen played an important part in rural life. Here are Reg Hannam and his son in 1942 with an Isle of Wight Creameries horse-drawn milk float.

These photographs are believed to be the work of J.Milne, photographer and seismologist, taken in 1901. They show pipe laying at Wroxall water works.

'Art' Moses with his horse in 1931. He is carrying buckets with the aid of a yoke and making his way home from the fields at Springfields Farm in Wroxall.

In 1922 most roads were of gravelled tar pressed into place by a steam roller. This gravelling gang are pictured at Yard Farm.

George ('Jolly') Saunders, haymaking at Gatcombe in 1917.

This portrait of George ('Jolly') Saunders in 1918 shows the true character of the British farmer.

Jacob Saunders, Will Hunt and Jim Dyer in 1940 with their threshing machine at Southford Farm, Whitwell.

In 1969 four cottages in Southford Lane, Redhill, were forced to share one well. Every summer the residents hoped the authorities would lay on mains water, but the argument was over cost and who would pay. Meanwhile, residents like Mrs Newington had to rely on buckets on a rope to raise water from a depth of 20ft.

Fred Kempton of Whitwell puts his shire horse through his paces prior to a ploughing match in 1957.

Northwood Cricket Club pavilion being re-thatched in 1928. It was destroyed in an air raid during World War Two.

The Hunt of Godshill in the 1960s, with village constable Phil Thatcher following the hounds on his bicycle. Constable Thatcher was one of the country's longest-serving village policemen who spent the whole of his service in Godshill with the exception of a small break for war service. He retired in 1970.

Blackgang Chine

Walter Dabell in 1890 and the son of Alexander Dabell, founder of Blackgang Chine, the world's first 'theme park'. Alexander died in 1898 and one year later Walter and his brother Francis joined the staff.

These staff at Blackgang Chine in 1920 included Mrs Isolene Dabell and her three lady helpers. The elderly gent is Bert Coles, head gardener at the Chine, and the tall man on the left his assistant. This was the entire staff of Blackgang Chine in those days.

In the early days of Blackgang Chine, Alexander Dabell established tea rooms which became popular with Sunday strollers. This picture was taken in 1890.

In the late 1800s a beautiful fin whale died when washed up on the beach at Alum Bay. Alexander Dabell bought it and bleached the bones which quickly took their place at the chine entrance. Here in 1890, the gift shop is seen inside the skeleton.

A view from Blackgang Chine taken in the 1950s and looking towards Freshwater Bay. Since then, due to massive cliff erosion caused by blue slipper mud, this panorama has altered considerably.

A view taken in 1904 and looking up the gorge to the entrance to Blackgang Chine.

A closer view of the
Blackgang Chine Gorge in the
1920s.

The Great Dinosaur Lift in 1971. This
is how the event has been known ever
since. The directors of the theme park,
realising the potential of growing
interest in dinosaurs and fossil
hunting, created a Dinosaur Park. The
scaled-down models were lifted into
their positions at Blackgang Chine by
helicopter.

The Undercliff slip at Windy Corner, Blackgang in September 1928 when an estimated 100,000 tons of rock cascaded down the cliff.

An 1883 picture, from a glass plate negative, of the road at Windy Corner, Blackgang.

Transport

The *Ryde Queen* on her moorings at Binfield. At one time she was a thriving night club but now, a disused rotting hulk.

The tug *Dwulia* towing the *Medway Queen* through the mouth of the River Medina on her way to her moorings at Cowes Haven, Binfield, in 1964.

Exterior of Cowes railway station at the junction of Terminus Road and Carvel Lane.

Train arriving at Mill Hill station from Cowes.

Newport Quay in 1909, showing coal barges waiting to be unloaded.

Mr Whittington, stationmaster, awaits the arrival of the up-train at Newchurch station in 1910.

The morning crew pose with their engine on 13 September 1952 on the last day of Ventnor West station.

Daish's stagecoach loaded for its journey from Shanklin to Ventnor.

Vectis buses at their depot at Sommerton Airport, Cowes, in 1921.

The latest in bus design acquired by Southern Vectis Bus Co and pictured at Freshwater in May 1936.

Shanklin bus station prior to its demolition in the 1980s.

Ventnor bus depot in July 1959.

The *Old Times* stagecoach *en route* from Arreton to Lake and Sandown.

A stagecoach loaded and ready to leave Sandown High Street.

RMS Olympic passing the Royal Yacht Squadron at Cowes in 1932. The *Olympic* was sister ship to the ill-fated *Titanic*.

The East to West Cowes chain ferry at East Cowes.

The *Havenstreet Queen* under a full head of steam proceeds along Yarmouth Quay.

The *Bat Boat*, built in 1912 by Saunders Roe of East Cowes. This was their first amphibious aircraft.

In the early part of the century this Bristol Box Kite aircraft made an emergency landing on Ventnor Downs. Many of the townsfolk turned out to help carry it to safety.

The Saunders Roe *Princess* flying boat over Alum Bay in 1952.

SRN 1, the first hovercraft, being put through her paces on a test run at East Cowes in 1959.

One of the early amphibious planes which Saunders built at East Cowes and supplied to the RAF was the London flying boat. In this picture three such aircraft are seen in formation over Cowes.

Built before its time by Saunders Roe was the *SRA 1*, a jet-powered amphibious flying boat, pictured being put through its paces at Cowes in 1947.

One of the more famous helicopters to be made at East Cowes by Saunders Roe was the *Skeeter*.

Carriages awaiting passengers at Freshwater railway station in 1908.

The 1920s saw the boom of the charabanc outing. Pictured is a typical pub party about to take to the road.

The Southern Vectis Bus awaiting passengers *en route* to Freshwater in the 1940s.

It only took a thin covering of snow on The Broadway, Totland, in 1953 to bring disaster to a Southern Vectis Bus. Luckily no serious injuries were sustained.

The Town Hall, Ryde, stands proudly unchanged since its foundation stone was laid in 1830.

Fountain Pier in 1899. This is known locally as Cowes Pontoon.

The driver of an open-top bus crowded with trippers pulls over to allow passengers to view the *QE2* on her passage through the Solent.

Shipwrecks

The schooner *Prim* lost off Atherfield Ledge on 22 February 1912.

SS Varvassi, a Greek steamer of 4,000 tons, en route from Algiers to Southampton, went aground on the rocks at The Needles in 1947. She eventually broke up and sank and her remains have been a noted navigational hazard.

The Dutch motor vessel *Volkerak* foundering off Blackgang in March 1951. The crew were rescued by Blackgang Life Saving Association.

In 1978, *Tarpenbek*, a tanker on the way to Fawley, ran into trouble east of the Nab. She was towed into the comparative calm of Sandown Bay where she remained half capsized for two weeks. Eventually she was righted and towed away for major repairs. This happened in 1978 and the locals had a field day selling T-shirts and other souvenirs.

While in use as a night club in 1981 the *Medway Queen* sank at her moorings Binfield. She was salvaged in 1983 and towed to Chatham.

Luigi Accame, a 500-ton Italian steamer, ran aground at Rocken End Blackgang on 6 April 1937. All the crew were saved by Yarmouth lifeboat and the ship was later successfully refloated.

On 25 April 1908, *HMS Gladiator* a Royal Navy cruiser was returning from USA to Portsmouth through the Solent when she was in collision with the steam ship *St Paul* which rammed her starboard side. The weather was extremely misty and the narrowness of the channel at Hurst Point was thought to be to blame. *St Paul* managed to limp back to Southampton.

Gladiator was beached off Colwell and turned over. Seen here are pumping operations taking place. She was eventually refloated and scrapped. Some 27 people lost their lives in the incident and many ships' captains and good people of the area swear that *Gladiator* still steams along the Solent.

Seaside

Seaview suspension pier, built by the Caws family. It was 1,000ft long, but due to damage sustained in high winds it was demolished in the mid-1950s.

The southern end of Sandown sea front in the 1890s.

This photograph of Ventnor was taken from a glass plate negative dated 1908 by Dore, a friend of J.Stephenson, photographer and seismologist.

Shanklin Esplanade in the mid-1880s, prior to the construction of the pier.

Ventnor beach in the early 1900s, showing the distinction between ladies and gentlemen's bathing huts.

Shanklin Pier and Esplanade at high tide, showing the bathing huts pulled as near to the sea wall as possible.

Sandown beach in 1926.

This whale was washed up on the beach at Atherfield on 16 May 1924 and measured 45ft in length.

The Esplanade, Sandown, in 1905.

Ventnor town, photographed from the pier by J.Dore in 1900.

Shanklin Esplanade and sea front, a picture believed to have been taken in 1900.

Steephill Cove in
1865, from a glass
plate.

Mackerel fishermen at
work off Wheelers Bay in
1910.

Ventnor Pier and Esplanade in 1891, a photograph taken from a boat.

The junction of Egypt Hill and The Esplanade at Cowes in 1910.

The old Cowes Green, *c.*1910, showing the Flora Statue.

Victoria Pier at Cowes was home to many shows and amusements.

This photograph of Cowes Pier, taken from the sea, shows the imposing Victorian terrace of houses which were demolished in 1929.

For years, mariners have been protected from the rock formation known as The Needles by the lighthouse built into the outer rock.

Freshwater Bay. It was here that Alfred Lord Tennyson, Poet Laureate, was to make his home at Farringford House, now a country hotel.

Totland Bay in the 1890s, then a popular bathing beach but now, unfortunately falling into decline.

Yarmouth Quay before the alterations in the 1980s.

The Arch Rock, Freshwater Bay, was a well-known landmark to mariners and visitors alike, but in the tides and gales of 1992 it succumbed to years of erosion and fell. All that is remains is the base rock.

Sport

Newport Cricket Club team in 1904. Back row (left to right): E.Mouncher (umpire), P.Shergold, W.Nobbs, A.Hame, P.Jefferies, F.Moore, S.Griffin (scorer). Front row: A.Stephenson, P.Damant, C.Howell, A.White, A.Watson, J.C.W.Damant.

East Cowes Nomads in the 1944-45 season. Pictured are Calton, Marvin, Riddell, Grant, Jones, South, Harvey, Butler, Woolwebber, Bracegirdle.

Godshill Cricket Club in 1962. Back row (left to right): R.W.Mew, H.Charles, N.Thorne, B.Thatcher, K.Day, G.R.Thorne, C.Hayles, A.Domoney. Front row: G.H.Thorne, R.Blow, D.J.Charles (captain), C.Thatcher, A.Mackett.

Godshill tug-of-war team in 1947. Isle of Wight heavyweight champions. Included are Reg Andrews, Percy Scott, Phil Thatcher and Art Cheverton.

Apse Heath Social Club with their trophies. Pictured are Messrs Denness, Hargreaves, Smith, Groves, Sibbick, Lavers, Tibbles, Morris, Guy and Barton.

Apse Heath Football Club in 1936. Back row (left to right): Guy, Sibbick, Driver. Middle row: Young, Stallard, McDonald. Front row: Holbrook, Mew, Whitlock, Brown, Whittington.

Newchurch footballers in 1946-47. Amongst those pictured are Lavers, Francis, Taylor, Moody, Stallard, Hayden, Russell, Austin, Hargreaves, Stephens.

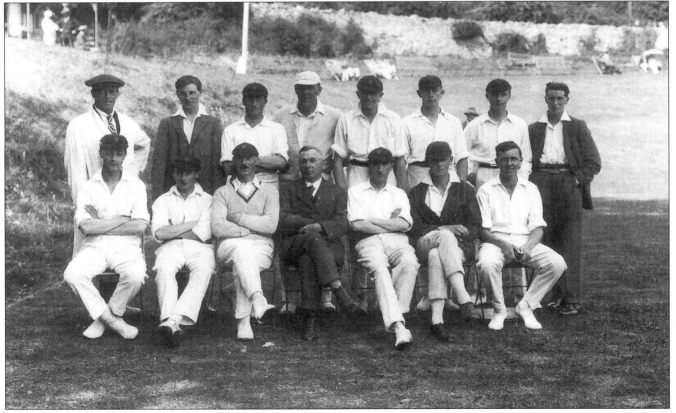

Ventnor Cricket Club in 1926. Back row (left to right): A.Moorman (umpire), Nelson Lowe, George Brading, H.Bert, Len Lacey, Howard Brading, J.C.Rogers, Charles Nigh. Front row: Albert Buckett, Charlie Foxworthy, Vic Howell, Mr Beasley (president), Toby Hills, Ralph Eldridge, Ralph Feaber.

The opening day of the Ventnor cricket pavilion.

West Wight Football Club, 1951-52 season. Back row (left to right): H.Read, B.Groves, R.Gregory, Maitland, Gregory, Evans, Clarke, H.R.Read, Woodford, Thompson, Beecham. Front row: Raish, Carter, Oliver, Hughes, Groves.

West Wight Social Club FC in 1932-33, when they were Western Division champions.

Godshill Cricket Club in 1964. Back row (left to right): G.Thorne, T.Jones, K.Day, C.Thatcher, B.Thatcher, R.Mew, L.Barlow, V.Radcliffe, P.Domoney (scorer). Front row: D.Charles, R.Blow, G.R.Thorne, D.J.Childs (captain), C.Hayles, A.Mackett, R.Denness.

Ventnor Cricket Club, season 1930. Back row (left to right): W.Lowe (umpire), L.Hess (honorary secretary), A.V.Howell, F.Burnett, W.Williams (scorer), W.Walker, N.V.Lowe. Front row: S.Locke, B.Bone, W.G.Mitchell (president), Dr L.G.Blair (captain), A.Dyer, W.J.Knight, H.C.Brading.

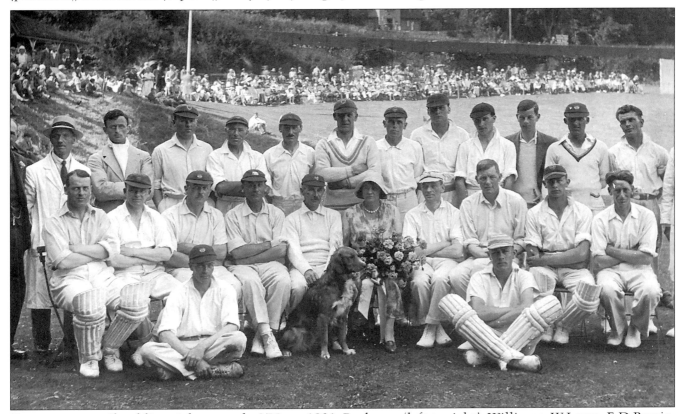

Ventnor versus Shanklin cricket match, 27 June 1931. Back row (left to right): Williams, W.Lowe, E.D.Bowie, W.J.Knight, B.Bone, E.V.Howell, J.B.White, A.Dyer, S.Locke, N.V.Lowe, F.Craddock, A.Cook, F.Griffiths, R.Warder. Middle row: A.R.Gibbon, L.Williams, A.Cook (captain of Shanklin), J.V.Hobbs, W.G.Mitchell, Mrs J.V.Hobbs (president), Dr L.G.Blair (captain of Ventnor), Revd A.A.P.Winser, H.C.Brading, S.Penfold. Front row: L.Marshall, E.Rice.

Ventnor Cricket Club 1st XI. Unfortunately we are unable to date this picture. Back row (left to right): R.Read (umpire), W.Bowe, W.Pound, E.Elgar, C.H.Denness (umpire). Middle row: W.Jeffrey, G.H.S.Saunders, Dr V.J.Balke (captain), J.Morgan Richards (president), H.Greenhalgh (vice-captain), W.G.Mitchell, F.C.V.Smith (honorary secretary). Front row: D.Day, A.E.Batt.

Ventnor Cricket Club in 1908, winners of the JH League. Back row (left to right): F.Dyer, J.M. de Vine, Mr Gordon, S.Moorman, Mr Adcock, H.Jeffery, G.Torey. Middle row: F.C.Y.Smith, Revd G.F.Langford, W.Mew Judd, H.Greenhalgh, Dr Blake. Front row: H.Lincoln, W.G.Mitchell.

Thrust, a jet-powered car, being wheeled from its garage at Fishbourne. Built by Richard Noble at Fishbourne, *Thrust* gained the land speed record in the USA a few years ago. It is pictured here with John Ackroyd and the team.